JOSHUA –
WARRIOR FOR GOD

Stephanie Jeffs

Illustrations by Colin Smithson

Scripture Union

Other titles in this series by Stephanie Jeffs
Jacob – wrestler for God
Elijah – champion for God
Peter – fisherman for God

Copyright © Stephanie Jeffs 2001
First published 2001

Scripture Union, 207–209 Queensway, Bletchley,
Milton Keynes, MK2 2EB, England.

ISBN 1 85999 451 2

British Library Cataloguing-in-Publication Data.
A catalogue record of this book is available from the British
Library.

Printed and bound in Great Britain by Creative Print and
Design (Wales) Ebbw Vale.

Chapter One

Looks can be misleading, can't they? I mean, you can look at a person and think how cool and calm they are, or how strong and tough. But that's not necessarily right, is it? Take me, for instance. I know that I look strong and tough. Well, I am strong and tough. Sometimes. I can hold my own. I can fight. And I can win. I look like a leader, which is just as well really, because that's what I am. But inside, inside it can be a bit different, scary even.

That's not being weak. It's just being honest. And I suppose if I didn't admit to feeling like this, I wouldn't know just how much God can help me and give me the strength I need.

It's not easy being a leader. And I should know! I've spent enough time backing up Moses to know how difficult it is, especially being leader of *this* lot. They just don't do what they're told. They like to think they know best. They still think like this – even after wandering around the wilderness for forty years.

Anyway, times change. New things happen – and I am one of the new things! The new leader. That's me. Even though I've been around for quite a long time, everyone sees me as the new boy. And now everyone is looking to me to do something. It's a bit scary, I can tell you.

Just look at the massive variety of tents sprawled out across the plain in front of me. Big tents, small tents, oddly-shaped tents. Every sort of tent you could possibly imagine. Some for the men and some for the women, but not a single person in sight. Everyone is in their own tent, doing their own thing, waiting to hear what I have to say, waiting to hear me speak. I can feel it. I can feel them waiting. We've spent thirty days mourning for Moses, but he's dead, and nothing is going to change that. And here we are, right on the edge of the land God has promised to give us. Everyone is waiting, looking at me to find out what's going to happen next. Well, they'll just have to wait a bit longer. I don't have a clue.

Actually that's not true. I *do* have a clue. I've already been into the Promised Land, just once. It was more than forty years ago, when I was young. Moses sent twelve of us out on a mission. We had to go into Canaan and find out everything we could: what the soil was like, what sort of crops grew well, what sort of people lived there and how they lived. Were their cities well defended? That sort of thing. Moses was very thorough; he wanted to know about everything. He was also fair. He chose one spy from each of the twelve tribes, so that everyone was represented.

Anyway, off we went. We did everything that Moses told us. We found out that the cities were very well defended, built on the top of hills, with big strong walls surrounding them. And there were some very tough looking people about. But the soil! Wow! I've never seen grapes like it. We cut off one cluster from a branch and it took two of us to carry it back! They were enormous. It was clear that Canaan would be a great place to live. Caleb and I didn't have any worries about it at all.

But when we got back to base and made our report to Moses and his brother Aaron, things didn't turn out how I expected. Everyone from the twelve tribes was there, waiting to hear what we had to say. No one listened to Caleb or me – the ten other spies just told the horror stories. "They're stronger than we are!" they said. "If we tried to fight them we'd be like little grasshoppers leaping around ready for a tribe of giants to stamp on us and squash us flat! We don't want to go to the Promised Land. It's too dangerous."

You can imagine what happened next. Panic broke out. Talk about grumbling and moaning. I'd never heard anything like it – and I've heard some whingeing in my time, I can tell you.

"We don't want to go to the Promised Land. We want to go back to Egypt. We were better off in Egypt even though we were slaves. Actually we'd be better off dead. Or in the desert!"

What could Moses do? Caleb managed to silence the crowd for a moment. "We can do it!" he yelled over the moans. "We can conquer Canaan. With God on our side you know we can! We can't lose!"

But that didn't work. They just didn't want to listen. Caleb and I tried as hard as we could to tell them about the good things we had seen in Canaan – huge grapes, a land flowing with milk and honey, but... Nobody listened. They just got more and more angry.

In the end it all got out of hand. They began to threaten us, picking up stones. Murder was in the air. At that point things were well out of control. I was afraid. It was crazy!

Then suddenly the most amazing thing happened. I'll never forget it as long as I live. Just to think about it makes me feel all shivery and weak at the knees. Something happened at the tent of the Meeting Place. A cloud came down and filled it. But it wasn't an ordinary cloud, it was a shimmering haze, like the brilliant rays from the sun or the misty aurora of the moon on a cold, clear night. It dazzled and shone. Everything stopped: all the moaning and the groaning and the anger. It all stopped. We all knew God had come down right in the middle of us all. He'd come to sort us out.

At first God was very angry. "How long will my people refuse to believe in me?" he said to Moses. "I promised to give them Canaan, but they refuse to believe me."

I shall never forget what Moses said to God. He didn't say what a moaning lot of whingers they all were and how they deserved whatever punishment God gave them and how they'd given him such a hard time. No! Instead Moses asked God to forgive them. *Forgive* them! And that's exactly what God did.

I know, all of that happened a long time ago. But you know what they say about leopards never changing their spots! Because now, everyone is waiting to listen to me.

The sun is just peeping over the horizon. A brand new day. What will happen today? More waiting? Or something else?

Slowly the camp comes to life. People are milling about, making bread, collecting water. I can see Mount Nebo in the distance, where Moses died. There's a good view from up there, right across the River Jordan into Canaan, the Promised Land.

Suddenly I feel someone touch me, and I swing round. But there is no one there. I must have imagined it! I am completely alone.

A gentle breeze swirls round me, and I

swing round again. Then I hear a voice. A whisper. "Joshua," it says.

Every hair on the back of my neck is standing to attention! It takes a while, but then of course I realise. I felt exactly the same when Moses put both of his hands on me and told me I was going to take over when he died, to be the Israelites' next leader. It's the Lord God. He wants to speak to me.

Chapter Two

"Get ready to go across the River Jordan and into the land of Canaan," said God. "I promised Moses that I would give the Israelites this land and I give you the same promise. Be brave! Be courageous! Don't be afraid or give up! I will be with you every step of the way! Do what I say and everything will go well!"

I took a deep breath. Funny really, but suddenly I knew what I had to say to the people. And as I looked across the flat plain, over the rolling waters of the River Jordan to the Promised Land of Canaan, I really did feel brave. I knew that God was with me.

"Officers!" I shouted.

They soon came scurrying. They looked at me. "Yes?"

"In three days' time we're going to cross the River Jordan and go into Canaan. Tell everyone to start packing, so that they'll be ready to move, when I give the orders."

I looked at each of my officers. I saw their faces looking up at mine, and I suddenly knew that they understood that I was in charge and that God was with me. "D'you understand?" I said firmly.

"Yes sir!" said one officer. "We'll do whatever you want, sir!"

Oh yes. I could tell they knew I was boss. I was beginning to feel really good. Confident even. God had made me a promise and I knew it was going to be all right.

"We'll obey you just like we obeyed Moses, sir!" said a third young officer.

"Thanks!" I said, trying not to sound too sarcastic. What a joke! I wanted obedience, but not like that. Moses had a hard struggle to get anyone to obey him for long. I looked at the officer. He was young. I hoped he was trying to be helpful.

"Dismissed!" I said.

I watched the officers go. I heard them barking out my orders to the people – and much to my surprise they actually obeyed them! I could tell just by watching. Everyone suddenly started to rush around.

Maybe things are going to change, I thought. Maybe we are going to change from being a group of people, all doing our own thing, into a lean mean fighting machine, ready to lead an invasion. Hard to believe, but not impossible. No, not impossible, just incredible.

I looked across the Jordan into Canaan. The sun was bright, and I shielded my eyes from the glare. Right in the distance I could just about make out the walls of Jericho. I didn't have to be close to them to see how big and thick they were. The city looked enormous even from a distance, built on a hill, surrounded by ramparts.

I sighed. Jericho! Taking over Jericho would not be easy. My confidence began to drain out of me, like wine seeping out of a cracked wine-skin. I was really no different from those ten spies all those years before.

Suddenly I had an idea! Spies! Of course that was it! Get to know your enemy before you panic, Joshua, I said to myself.

Then I muttered aloud. "I'll send two spies into Jericho. I'll find out exactly what we're up against!"

Chapter Three

"Well?" I whispered. Several days had passed since the spies had left us and now we were well away from the camp, but even so, I didn't want anyone else to hear, just in case. I remembered only too well how spies caused panic. I didn't want anything to happen like that, this time. I turned to one of them. "What did you find out?"

"Well the good news is that we got into Jericho," he replied.

"And the bad news is we nearly got caught!" said the other.

"What?!!" I exploded. This is a great start, I thought. If we have trouble getting two people in and out of Jericho how will we cope with a whole nation traipsing through?

"It's all right, sir," said the first spy. "It all happened for the best, I'm sure of it!"

I breathed a sigh of relief. Be bold! Be strong! Don't give up! I was sure I heard the words whispered in my head.

"Go on," I said, listening hard.

It was a strange story. The spies had managed to get into Jericho. No mean feat in itself. Apparently everyone was very twitchy. The spies had found themselves in a house belonging to a woman called Rahab, whose home was right in the city walls. A good place to find out what was happening, and to spot any comings or goings, in or out of the city.

Of course they'd soon been discovered. The Jericho intelligence service is good. They know that we are camped on the edge of the Jordan, waiting to invade. The king of Jericho gets daily reports and the whole city is on red alert, on the look-out for anyone or anything strange! So, the spies were soon noticed and men were sent to find them. "But the people are afraid," said one of the spies. "They're afraid, because they know that the Lord God is on our side. They've heard all about the plagues in Egypt, and how in the end Pharaoh was begging us to leave, so that he could be rid of us. They've heard how Moses held out his staff across the Red Sea and how the waters rolled back like a carpet to let us through. And they've heard how the entire Egyptian army were drowned once they tried to cross. They've heard about everything that has happened to us, and they're very, very scared."

"Anyway sir," continued the other. "Just when we thought we were done for, Rahab hid us on the roof of her house, under some stalks of flax. They weren't half heavy. Then, when the coast was clear we shinned down a rope from her window."

"And, I hope you don't mind sir, but as she saved our lives we promised to save her and her family, if we conquer the city."

"*If?*" I said, surprised by my own reaction.

"Not *if*, but *when*. *When* we conquer Jericho, Rahab and her family will be spared!"

Chapter Four

It's funny how much can change in a few days. A few days ago I didn't really know how we were going to get into Canaan. Now I knew not only how we were going to get into Canaan, but I was quite sure that the first thing we would do when we got there was to march to Jericho. Canaan! For the last forty years the one subject that always cropped up was Canaan. When was God going to take us to Canaan? How would we get there? Getting to Canaan was the reason God had rescued us from Egypt. In fact, getting to Canaan was the reason for most of the things that had happened to us as a nation, ever since God had first spoken to Abraham, hundreds and hundreds of years ago. And now it looked like it was finally going to happen. We were going to Canaan!

Of course, before we reached Canaan there was one small problem. Well, a rather big problem actually, And a wet one. The River Jordan. Not only was the River Jordan a big river, and a wide river, it was also flowing very fast because it was a flooding river.

But of course, I should have known. God had got the whole thing sorted. He had a plan and all I had to do was to make sure that it was carried out.

"Get the people ready!" I said to my officers.

"They've been on stand-by for a while now, sir," said one.

"Well there's ready and ready," I said smartly. I could tell he didn't have a clue what I was talking about. "There's ready in the packing up sense, and there's ready in the inside sense!"

"Sir?"

"Look! This is a big moment for us! Perhaps the biggest moment our people have ever known. God is going to lead us into the land he promised to give Abraham hundreds and hundreds of years ago. Babies have been born, people have died, we escaped from being slaves in Egypt, and now finally *we* – you and me and all those people out there – are going to do it! We're actually going to do it! We are going to enter God's Promised Land! So..."

I don't think I took a breath. It all came out in such a rush. But as I spoke I suddenly realised what an amazing thing we were going to do. It was as if what we were about to do was going to change history, and stand out as *the* moment in time for us as God's people. Everything was poised, pointing to this moment, the moment when everything that God had ever promised, all his plans for the future were coming true. It was such a moment that this time we had to get it right. There could be no room for error. We had to be ready, absolutely completely and utterly ready.

"So..." I continued. "I think everyone needs to get ready. In other words we need to get our lives ready to step into God's Promised Land. We need to make sure that we leave behind the things that belong to the past, the moanings and the groanings and the disobedience so that this is a new start, with nothing to spoil it. We must make sure that we have spoken to God, and said sorry to him, so that we are ready to go into this special place."

"Yes sir!" shouted the officers, before marching through the camp.

The officer marched off, but I hardly saw him go. I felt a weight pressing down on me, as if the enormity of everything that I'd just thought and said was about to crush me. And I realised how much I meant what I said. We needed to say sorry to God. We'd done so many bad and wicked things over the years. We'd sinned – me as well. We'd all offended God in some way or other. We were all the same.

Men, women and children made their way from the camp to the big tent, set a little way away. It was the tent of the Meeting Place, a special place, God's home with us.

It didn't take long before a strange hush descended. Everything went quiet and still. The only thing that happened was the gentle breeze that sighed round me.

"Lord God," I whispered into the breeze. "Forgive us. Forgive me. Make us ready. Make me ready. Please."

Chapter Five

Amazing! God had given me a plan! I knew *the* plan, God's plan. God had told me. And I knew it was amazing. God didn't have to tell me how amazing it was. I just knew it!

I told the people what to do. I only hoped that they had listened. And that they would do what I had said.

There were people everywhere, hundreds and thousands of them. Like a colony of ants, moving forwards. Men, women and children – all from different tribes, all clutching their possessions, all ready to go. At least I hoped so.

Nobody spoke. Everyone was waiting.

Suddenly the twelve priests walked forwards carrying the Ark of the Covenant. Everyone gasped. Some fell on their knees. Others shielded their eyes from the brilliant glare. It was so beautiful. So holy. It was God's special place, a sign that God is with us. The golden box flashed and gleamed in the sunlight. It looked as though it were alive, it was so beautiful. And as its beam bounced and glowed, shedding its golden light across the faces of the people I thought of what it contained: the two stones God had given to Moses, on which were written God's laws, the way he wanted his people to live.

Slowly the priests walked forwards towards the deep rushing waters of the River Jordan.

The people began to move. "Not too fast, not too fast," I said to myself. "Mind the Ark!" The Ark of the Covenant is so special that if the wrong person touches it there will be big trouble. But the people hung back. Just like I'd told them to.

I watched as the priests got nearer to the river. The sound of the water was immense. It poured downstream, gurgling and splashing and bubbling. It was fierce.

"Amazing!" I heard the voice speak once again in my ear. "You will see amazing things today."

"Amazing things!" I said aloud. And as I

did so I watched the priests carry the Ark into the river.

As soon as the first priest put his foot into the river, the noise stopped. A strange silence engulfed us and overwhelmed us, and once again I felt tiny shivers tip-toeing up and down the bones in my back, while the hairs on the back of my neck tingled in anticipation. The quietness and the stillness froze us in time. And then I noticed what had happened. The water had stopped. The River Jordan had stopped flowing downstream.

Everyone gasped again. I felt as though I wanted to cheer, "Hurrah for the Lord God!" but I thought better of it. I was the leader after all. But I really wanted to. It was so amazing. One moment there was a big flooding river. The next, there was half a river flowing off in the distance, and a clear path right across to Canaan.

Now there was no doubt in anyone's mind that God had done something very special.

As soon as the priests reached the middle of the river bed, I gave my order. I nodded at an officer and he nodded at the people, and they all picked up their things and walked across the river bed to the other side.

That was amazing too! Everyone just did it. No one asked any questions or made alternative suggestions. We just walked across past the Ark of the Covenant, into the Promised Land of Canaan.

Chapter Six

When I crossed the river I couldn't help myself!

"Yes!" I said and flung my fist in the air. "Let's hear it for the one and only, amazing Lord God almighty!"

But nobody heard me.

Nobody heard me, because once we reached the other side and their feet touched the Promised Land of Canaan, everyone started to speak at once.

Everyone hugged and kissed each other. They smiled and laughed. Women and children danced and sang and the men slapped one another on the back and said things like, "We never thought we'd see this day!" and "Did you ever see anything like it? It must have been like the time my gran crossed the Red Sea with Moses!"

There was a real party. Occasionally someone remembered to say something good about God.

And all the time the priests were standing in the river bed, holding the Ark of the Covenant. Not easy, I can tell you. The Ark is very special and incredibly holy, and it's also very heavy.

"Joshua!"

I turned round. It was old Seth. A nice old man. "What a day!" he gasped. "I shall never forget it as long as I live! This is a day to remember for ever. It's the sort of day I heard my grandparents talk about, but I never thought I'd see such things for myself."

"Me neither," I said, and put my arm round his shoulder. "I shouldn't think any of us will forget!"

"Oh yes they will!"

I let go of Seth and turned around. There was no one there. Just that gentle breeze in my face.

"People do forget!" said the Lord God quite clearly in my ear. "I should know! They forget me often enough. But I have a plan that will help them remember!"

I listened carefully to the next stage in

God's plan.

"Right!" I said, as soon as the last person had crossed the river. "We've done it! God's done it! We've invaded! The conquest has begun!"

Chapter Seven

I listened as a murmur of excitement rippled through the people. I could tell they felt more confident about what was ahead. They had seen God act. We had all seen God's power.

"But," I said firmly, waiting for silence. "Before we can move on, this is what God wants us to do. He wants us to remember what he has done for us today!"

"We will! We will!" shouted the crowd. I looked at them all. There were thousands of them. And every single one of them was completely and utterly dry. There wasn't a drip of water anywhere. Amazing!

"*We* might!" I shouted back. "Our children might just, but their children probably won't. So... I want each tribe to choose one of their strongest men..."

I soon had twelve men standing in front of me. They certainly looked big and tough. They needed to be.

"Now each one of you is to go back into the river bed and pick out a huge stone. When we make camp tonight we'll put them up and leave them there. It will be a reminder of all the amazing things God has done for us, especially today, and then we can tell our children and our grandchildren about it."

The men heaved the stones out of the river bed, and carried them back to dry land. Once they were safely on the other side, the priests carried the Ark of the Covenant out

from the river bed and into the Promised Land of Canaan.

Then a strange thing happened. First there was a murmuring in the distance like the sound of pebbles on the sea shore. Then the murmuring grew louder and louder until it turned into a roar, and a million stones scattered down the river bed, pushed on by a great wall of water. The river began to flood again, just as it had done before.

And I suddenly wondered what the people living along the River Jordan had made of it all. What did they think had happened? Could they even begin to guess that God was doing something? One moment they'd been living alongside a busy river, and the next moment it had completely dried up. At least they would know that we'd arrived and that God was on our side. Although I was quite sure they would not like it!

I looked back over the Jordan, into the desert. Forty years we'd spent wandering around the desert, and now we'd finally arrived. But of course we weren't home and dry yet. Well – we were dry! And I suppose we were home. Well, sort of. But God hadn't just promised that we would cross over the River Jordan and step into Canaan. He'd promised to give us the whole land. Every last bit of it.

The only problem was that there were other people living there already. And they weren't so keen for us to have it. And they weren't about to give it away. We'd have to fight for it.

The sun was beginning to go down, casting long shadows throughout the camp, and over the twelve huge stones. Menacing shadows. Just like the enemies I knew were lying in wait for us, with all their strange names and customs, and their gods. Their gods made of stone and wood; their gods who controlled their fortunes – or so they believed. Their gods and their idols. A picture of the two stone tablets resting in the golden Ark flashed before my mind. "You shall not worship any other God but me!"

Oh yes – we had entered the Promised Land, but we had also entered unknown dangerous territory, I was sure of that.

And as evening came, I couldn't help wondering what God had in store for us next.

Chapter Eight

The early morning sun shone brightly. I leapt off my bedding roll. I didn't need more sleep. I was raring to go.

I looked back across the Jordan and watched the rapid water twisting its way downstream. I laughed – I couldn't help it. If I hadn't seen it with my own eyes I'd have found it hard to believe that we had crossed that river in the way we did. I smiled to myself, just thinking about the rumours that must have swept through Canaan as rapidly as the waters flowed now. "The Israelites are coming! The Israelites are coming! And the Living God is with them."

"He sure is!" I said out loud. "And you'd better watch out!"

The golden glow of the sun warmed me, and I turned to look ahead. The camp was quiet and still. Everyone was asleep. "Too much good food!" I thought and patted my stomach contentedly.

Yes, things had certainly looked up since we crossed the Jordan. We'd only just entered the Promised Land and already things were good. I tried not to think, I told you so! but I couldn't help it. And anyway it was true! I *had* told everyone so! I had told them that the land of Canaan was brilliant and now they were beginning to see some of the evidence – and taste it too! The grain was so plump and tasty. The bread was delicious. And the fruit – well we hadn't tasted anything like it in years. All we'd had were manna and quail, quail and manna, manna and quail!

"Not that there was anything wrong with that!" I said hastily, casting a brief smile up to heaven. "But this is better!"

In fact we'd been grateful for the manna and quail. Otherwise we would have starved in the desert. There was nothing else to eat, and once again the people had muttered how much better things were in Egypt. At least then we'd had pomegranates and cucumbers. But, quite miraculously God *had* provided us with food. When we needed food, flocks of quail birds had arrived and hopped around the camp, just waiting to be eaten. And every morning flakes of manna lay like dew over the ground. Once the flakes had been gathered we could make bread.

But the funny thing was, once we had crossed over the Jordan and celebrated our first Passover meal in the Promised Land, the manna stopped. We didn't need it any more! There was plenty to eat in Canaan.

It took a little while to get used to, though. It was strange not waking up each morning and seeing the ground covered in white flakes. I'd almost forgotten what it was like to wake up and see everything as it was.

And now, as the sun continued to rise in the sky, a few people moved about the camp, collecting water, making fires, that sort of thing, getting ready for the day ahead.

I looked beyond the camp to the high mound in the distance. Jericho. Its strong, high walls towered over the horizon.

I needed a walk. I needed time to think. It had been good to make camp and rest awhile, but perhaps now was the time to make a move. After all, God had promised to give us the whole of the Promised Land of Canaan, not just the first few hundred metres!

I walked on, keeping my eyes fixed on Jericho's huge city walls. The further I walked, the larger and stronger the walls appeared to be.

I thought back to the meeting I had had with the spies! It all seemed such a long time ago. So much had happened since. But I had known then that we had to conquer Jericho, and so it was no surprise now.

We'll be all right! I thought to myself, and mentally I made a note of our fighting men. How many did we have? Thirty thousand? Fifty thousand? Thirty thousand good ones, anyway. That was a reasonable army. A very reasonable army.

But of course we didn't just have fighting men. We had women and children, babies and old people as well. We might have a fighting force, but we also had loads of people who couldn't do very much, and we had to take them with us as well.

Will it be all right? I found myself thinking, and I swung my foot and sent a shower of pebbles into the air.

Suddenly I stopped. I had been so busy thinking, I hadn't heard anyone coming. A man stood ahead of me, dressed like a warrior. In his hand he held a huge sword which glinted in the sunlight.

I gulped. The roof of my mouth went dry and my heart raced in my chest.

I stared at the man and he stared back at me. My arms were taut, ready for any sudden movement.

Neither of us spoke. We just stared. The man's eyes stared right through me, as if he had locked me in his gaze.

He'll move any moment now, I thought, and then I'll be done for!

I wondered how far I had wandered away from the camp. I wondered if I could shout loud enough to be heard. I wondered how quickly help could come – if I needed it.

I felt my mind clear, and the thumping in my chest grew quieter. But I never took my eyes off the man. And he never took his eyes off me – nor did he drop his sword.

I took a deep breath. "Who are you?" I shouted. "Are you a friend of the Israelites or are you our enemy? Friend or foe? Go on! Tell me who you are!"

"Neither!" shouted the man.

"What do you mean?" I replied. "You must be one or the other! You are either for us or for our enemies! Tell me which!"

"Neither!" replied the man again. "I am the commander of the Lord God's army. That is the reason I am here!"

Smack! It was as if someone had floored me, pushed me from behind. I just fell to the ground, without so much as a thought.

It was as if it was the only thing to do. The hairs on the back of my neck bristled and I felt a strange shimmer up and down my spine. I kept my face to the ground. I knew this person was special.

"Why have you come?" I asked, my mouth still touching the ground. My voice sounded strange, all shaky and quiet. "Have you a message for me?"

"Only this," said the man. "This place is holy. Take off your sandals!"

I didn't need to be asked twice! My fingers were already untying the thongs.

"But..." I continued, and I glanced up.

But the man had gone. There was no one there.

Slowly I stood up. I brushed the earth off my chest and wiped the mud from my face, checking all the time that the man had gone. And he had.

What on earth did he mean? I wiggled my toes and felt the earth squidge between them. It felt rich and warm and comforting.

"Holy ground!" I said out loud. I bent down and took a handful of earth. "This land, this earth is special. It's God's. It's holy. It's his to give to whom he wants. And he's promised it to us!"

With that I flung the earth into the air, picked up my sandals and made my way back to the camp.

Chapter Nine

We fixed our eyes on the high walls of the city. We watched for quite a while. But there was nothing much to see, because nothing went into Jericho and nothing came out. Just a bird or two, and the rats.

The huge city walls towered above us, and the great wooden gates remained tightly closed. Nothing stirred. Nothing moved.

I was sure the king of Jericho knew we were there. And I knew he was scared, very, very scared. He was ready for a siege. But he wasn't going to have one. I was fairly sure that once God started to work it would all be over quickly. All I had to do was to wait for God to give me the word – and tell me exactly what he wanted me to do.

I just kept watching. And waiting. How are we going to breach those walls? I thought to myself. Do we have enough weapons? How will we attack?

I really couldn't imagine, but I still couldn't stop my mind from turning over every possibility I could think of.

Suddenly the wind began to stir and change direction and I felt a gentle familiar breeze sweep across my face.

"Look at Jericho," whispered the voice in my ear. "It's tightly shut! The king of Jericho and all his soldiers are wrapped up, just like a parcel, ready for you to take."

I looked up at the city again. I'd never really thought of it like that before. Of course, God was exactly right. It was all just there, ready for us to take. A Jericho take-away. Only – I wasn't sure it was going to be that easy!

But... "How?" I whispered back to the voice in my ear. "How will we take the city?"

"March," said the voice.

"March?" I said.

"Yes, march," repeated the voice.

"March into the city?" I said, trying not to sound surprised. Could we really just march up to the city gates and ask to go in? I doubted it somehow.

"Not in," said the voice, "but *round*. Round and round the city walls. Tell seven priests to march around the city walls, in front of the Ark of the Covenant. They must each carry a trumpet. Then march your fighting men behind them. Do this once a day for six days."

"Right!" I said. "Once a day for six days. And then?"

"And then," said the voice, "I'll tell you exactly what to do on the seventh."

"I can't wait," I said.

And I meant it. I could hardly wait to see what God was going to do.

Chapter Ten

It took time to organise it, to get it all together. But by the end of the week we had got it down to a fine art.

The priests, dressed in white with their huge ram's horn trumpets slung round their necks, provided a sharp contrast to the rest of the men, a mixed bunch armed with swords and whatever weapons they could get their hands on.

Then there was the Ark. It may just look like a wooden box covered in gold, but it's far more than that too. The Ark lets everyone know that the Lord God is with us. The Living God is here, along with everything he wants us to do, because his laws are written on stone tablets and are kept inside the box, a sign that they are at the very centre, at the heart of everything God does.

"Ready?"

"Yes, sir!"

"You know what to do!" I shouted. It wasn't a question. Just a reminder that they had had their instructions.

"Yes, sir!" shouted the assembled crowd.

"Then move!"

I watched the procession head off around the city walls. The golden Ark caught the light and for a moment appeared full of its own movement and energy as the light danced over the wings of the two guardian angels which decorated the top.

Then followed the fighting men, at a safe distance from the Ark. They marched and they stomped. Whereas the Ark glimmered with liquid light, they looked fierce and mean.

I wondered how many enemy eyes were squinting through the shutters in the city walls.

"I bet they wonder what will happen next!" I said to one of my officers who was standing beside me. "Well, they'll just have to wait and see – they'll never be able to guess. No one could!"

After a while I saw the priests emerge from the other side of the city walls. Once they

were round, everyone could break ranks
and have a rest. That was it. That was all
God wanted us to do.

At least – that was all he wanted us to do,
for six days. But then there was day seven.

Chapter Eleven

Day Seven. The seventh day. This was it!

I was up early on day seven. I could hardly sleep. I felt nervous and excited at the same time. We all did. I looked at Jericho, with its thick strong walls, and took a deep breath.

Late last night I had given everyone their final briefing, making sure that everyone knew what was going to happen.

"The great thing with this battle plan is that we know how it will end!" I said. "So, if we do exactly what God says, we've got nothing to worry about!"

I saw a few faces smile, but most of the men looked nervous. There's nothing to worry about! I wanted to shout to them. The Living God is with us. We can't lose. But you can't just tell people. They have to find out for themselves.

I took another deep breath, held out my

arms and gave the signal for the procession to begin, for the very last time.

I watched as the priests set off around the city walls. But this time, instead of their trumpets swinging around their necks, they held them in their hands, lifted them up to their lips and started to blow!

The sound of the trumpet blast echoed and bounced round the city walls. It seemed to bounce off every brick. The sound completely surrounded and engulfed us.

"If that doesn't put the wind up them, nothing else will," I said to myself.

Once, twice, the priests circled the city walls. I kept my eyes fixed on the fortress, ready to detect any flicker, any movement. But there was nothing.

The priests continued to march. Three times, four times, five times. Still no movement came from the city, but the haunting tuneless blast from the trumpets continued to fill the air, with never a gap or a silence.

I smiled as the priests walked past. I was impressed. I never knew they had so much breath in them.

"Six," I counted to myself as the procession disappeared around the city walls. "Only one more round, and then... and then..."

I hardly dared think about it, even though God had told me what he was going to do. I had watched and I had waited for this moment – we all had – and now it was here. God was going to do something amazing, and we were going to see it happen.

I felt my heart pounding in my chest. I wondered how all the people inside the city were feeling, hearing the continuous blast from the trumpets, uncertain what was going to happen next. I knew they must be afraid. They had every reason to be.

"Mustn't forget Rahab," I said to myself as the priests appeared around the city walls, ready to make the circuit for the last time.

"Seven!" I said out loud, and raised my hand to talk to the people. There was an eerie silence and that strange hush descended as it had before when we crossed the Jordan. I could feel God's presence with us, holding us, surrounding us. Every nerve in my body felt alert, twitching with anticipation. The brilliance of the golden Ark flashed in the stillness, sending rays of golden rainbow light over us and over the mighty walls of Jericho.

"Listen everyone!" I ordered. "When I give the signal you are to shout, because God has given us victory already. The city of Jericho is ours!"

I almost expected a cheer to go up. But it didn't. I looked across at the sea of faces watching me. They looked gaunt and tense with anticipation. I could see some of them clearly sizing up the city walls. I could almost tell what they were thinking. "OK Joshua. It's all right for you to say that God has let us conquer Jericho, but from where I'm standing those city walls look as if they've been there for a very long time, and as if they're going to stay there for a very long time. In fact they look like a permanent feature. Tough and solid!" Well, they wouldn't have long to wait and see.

"Remember!" I said, letting my words echo around the company. "Remember what I told you. No one, *no one* is to take anything for themselves. Once we have entered the city, all the plunder, the gold and the silver, anything made of bronze or iron is God's. It must be put in the treasury! It belongs to God!"

I felt sure I'd made the point. There could be no misunderstanding otherwise we'd all be in trouble. Serious trouble.

"But first of all," I said, "we have to enter the city. Ready...?"

I lowered my hand and the priests drew a deep breath and blew on their trumpets.

I raised my other hand and pointed into the sky.

"AAAAAAAAAArrrrgggghhhh," shouted the people.

And above the sound of the trumpets and the roar, came a deep cracking sound!

Chapter Twelve

In the end it was all over very quickly. That sound stopped everyone in their tracks. We were all stunned by the sight of a crack running round the entire city walls, like a rip in a piece of cloth.

Then the whole wall splintered and toppled as if it were made of papyrus. Kaboom! Huge clouds of dust billowed into the sky.

We didn't wait for it to settle. I knew we were onto a winner. We all did! "Charge!" I roared.

"Chaaaarge!" roared the people and they rushed forwards, wielding their swords as they clambered over the city walls like horses at a chariot race.

I spotted a couple of my spies, just about to rush into Jericho. They were grinning from ear to ear.

"Cor!" said one. "I've never seen anything

like it! What a victory!"

"Remember Rahab," I said. "We've made promises to her which we must keep. Get into the city as quickly as you can and bring out everyone she has with her. It's up to you to make sure that they get out safely."

"Right!" they said and leapt into action.

I stood back for a while and watched. The sounds from the city were deafening. Shouts and cries. Whoops and yells. I knew what was happening in there. Nothing was to be spared. God had told me so.

I felt that strange shiver run up and down my back, and for a moment the excitement of the battle and the victory left me. "Lord God," I whispered in my head. "You are so great. How can we ever understand the things you do? You are so special. Holy, in fact. May we accept your holiness – and take you seriously."

I saw some people running, running away from the city: men, women and children. I shielded my eyes from the sun. I wanted to make sure they were the right people. Then I saw the spies with them. A woman walked between them, and I moved towards her.

Before I reached her she fell to the ground. "Thank you," she said, "for keeping me and my family safe."

"Thank you for saving my men's lives." I said to Rahab, taking her by the hand. "You are one of us now. You and your family will be safe with us."

"Safe with the Living God," said Rahab looking up at me.

"Yes," I said to her. "We are all safe when the Living God is with us."

I smelt smoke. Rahab scrambled to her feet. We turned to look at the city. It was on fire. Jericho was burning. Soon there would be nothing left. Jericho had fallen. We had won.

The Living God was on our side.

"Make sure all the gold, silver and bronze is put aside for God," I said to some men, who were dragging a large chest away from the smouldering city. "Those are God's orders. Remind everyone."

Flames rose from the ruins and black smoke scudded across the sky, like a charcoal stream gliding into the distance. I watched the smoke travel and saw charred embers floating on the wind. I had no idea how far they'd travel, but I knew that it wouldn't take long before all of Canaan would know what the black smoke meant. Jericho had fallen. Who would be next?

"God has destroyed Jericho!" I shouted. "No one is to rebuild it. Ever!"

Chapter Thirteen

I was really buzzing after Jericho. We all were. We felt invincible. There was nothing we could not do, no one we could not fight – and win! With God on our side, of course. Now there would be no stopping us.

And I didn't feel like stopping either. I was on a real roll – rolling straight from over the Jordan, right on through the Promised Land. "Watch out, everyone," I muttered under my breath as I looked across the horizon. "Watch out, Ai. We're comin' through!"

It wasn't just me. None of us felt like stopping. It was like we really, truly believed that this land was ours already. Even though we'd only conquered one city. Everything was going to be OK.

There was no shortage of volunteers to spy on Ai.

"Go and find out all about the city," I said, "and the surrounding area. I do like to know what we're up against."

Not that it really makes much difference, when God is working with you. But even so, as I said to my men, God has the plan and we have to obey his orders and do our bit.

They nodded in agreement. At last, I thought, we are finally grasping the fact that when we obey God everything ends up going well for us, and when we don't it can only mean trouble. Perhaps, at last, those days of disobedience and trouble are over and done with.

The spies didn't take long to suss out the land, and the city.

"It's a doddle!" they said.

"It'll be easy, compared with Jericho. No one who lives there is capable of putting up a good fight. We'll pulverise them in no time."

"Don't bother sending up too many men," said one of the spies. "Let the men stay here and have a rest. Just send up a couple of thousand. They'll be back in no time."

It was like music to my ears.

This is great, I thought to myself, and I

went up to pick out my troops.

I walked down the lines of fighting men, touching the chosen ones on the shoulder and letting the others return to the camp.

Actually, I was beginning to enjoy myself. For the first time I realised I was actually beginning to enjoy being the leader. I was really getting to grips with the job. "It's all about obedience," I said to myself and to God. "I can see that if we do as you say everything will go well. I think the people are starting to see that too. So I'm sure everything is going to be all right from now on, and you won't need to be angry with us any more."

I'd picked enough men. I didn't want to hang around. We all wanted to get going and get the thing over and done with.

"Come on, men!" I said, marching forwards. "Let's take Ai!"

A great cheer went up.

"Ai!" they shouted confidently.

Chapter Fourteen

We marched across the plains towards the city. It certainly didn't look as impressive as Jericho. I wondered how we would take it. I wondered what plan God had in mind. "Tell me what to do next!" I whispered into the wind. I could see the city gates in the distance. Perhaps we just knock on the door and ask to come in, I said to myself, smiling.

The wind suddenly changed direction and instead of the gentle breeze, I felt a blast of icy cold air rush into my face. I closed my eyes for a moment as dust rose in the air.

"Tell me..." I began.

"Look!" gasped a voice from behind me.

I looked.

As the dust the wind had churned up began to settle, I could see more dust rising in the distance. I heard the clatter and beat of horses' hooves as they pounded towards us.

I gulped. This didn't look right to me. There was a whole army charging right up to us. There were so many of them. They didn't look afraid of us. Not in the least bit. They looked as though they were going to give us more than a run for our money.

"What shall we do?"

I knew I had to give an order, but as I watched the galloping horses advancing towards us, my mind froze. This wasn't what I had expected. This wasn't supposed to happen.

"Fight!" I said, and I drew my sword. "And then retreat."

I could hardly believe I said the word. Retreat. It wasn't a word I used very often, and I hadn't expected to use it today. But today wasn't going as I had expected. Not at all.

The enemy army galloped towards us and rushed down on us, screaming and shouting. I swung out with my sword, listening to the clash of metal. I didn't look around. I just kept fighting, lashing out with my sword, stabbing and thrusting wildly at the enemy, my mind trying to block out the sounds of the screams and the pain, wondering whether the cries of agony were coming from my soldiers or our enemies. I kept going, waving my sword frantically, defending rather than attacking.

And then I retreated. I knew when we were losing. I knew it was no good prolonging the agony. As soon as I could, I escaped. I turned and made my way back to the camp.

Everyone was waiting for me. Standing in silence. Watching and waiting.

"What happened?" I said to one of my officers.

"They chased us away. They defeated us. We didn't get anywhere near the city."

"They were ready for us and they were better than us."

I pulled a face. I didn't want to hear things like that.

"How many dead?" I whispered.

"Thirty. Forty. Something like that."

I nodded and pounded my fist in the palm of my hand.

There was still silence. Then came the sound of muffled sobs, from those who were waiting for their men to return.

I knew what they were all thinking. *Joshua's got it wrong. We're done for. God's let us down.* I didn't have to ask them. I just knew. And the reason I knew was because, if I was honest, I was thinking the same things too. Had I got it wrong? What had we done? Where was God? Why had he let us down? Why had he let it happen?

There was only one way to find out.

I walked silently through the camp, towards the tent of the Meeting Place. I stood before the Ark of the Covenant.

"Come with me!" I said to the elders of each of the twelve tribes.

Then I took hold of my tunic, held it in my hands and ripped it. I ripped it again and again, from the neck, from the hem, until it was tattered. Then I threw myself onto the ground. I buried my face in the earth and grasped it with my fingers, digging my nails deep into the dirt.

"Why!" I said as I gripped the earth. Lord God! Why? Why did you let us be humiliated like this? Why did you bother to let us cross the River Jordan, if it was all going to end like this. Why did you let us have such a great time in Jericho, if we were going to lose such a small battle today. Why?" I screamed into the earth. The words tumbled through my mind and straight out of my mouth like an ugly torrent of grief, misery and rage. "Why? Why? Why?" And I banged the ground with my fists.

I let my feelings cool for a moment. Then

the tears came. They spurted out from my eyes and ran down my cheeks, before being soaked up by the earth. "It would have been better if we had never crossed the Jordan. We should have stayed where we were. Now everyone will laugh at us. All our enemies will soon be here. They'll have a field day! They'll easily destroy us!"

I felt the gush of words stop their flow. I'd shocked myself. I didn't know I felt like that. I never thought I'd talk to God like that either. Anyway, it didn't matter now. Nothing mattered now. We'd all be dead soon anyway. I screwed up my eyes and pressed my face into the mud.

"Stand up!"

It was not like a voice I had ever heard before. But I knew it was the voice of the Lord God. The sound of his order seemed to catapult me to my feet and I leapt up. My legs were shaking and my hands hung by my side, while my fingers quivered as the voice echoed round me.

I stood there. My eyes stared at the golden Ark, which glimmered and gleamed with such painful, searing brilliance, that I was forced to screw up my eyes and look away.

"What were you doing with your face on the ground?" The voice questioned. But I knew I wasn't expected to give an answer. I knew perfectly well that God knew exactly what I had been doing, lying on the ground and he didn't need me to explain it to him. He had seen me and he had heard every word I had said.

"You have sinned. All of you have sinned. My people, the Israelites, have disobeyed me."

My mind grew clearer. I tried to work out what God was saying. What had we done? I didn't know. I didn't have a clue. But whatever it was, we were all in serious trouble. Every single one of us.

"Sovereign Lord," I said looking straight at the Ark. I could feel God's presence hit me like a furnace, while small shivers ran their fingers up and down my spine. "What have we done?"

"My people have lied to me and they have stolen from me. They have kept some of the things which were mine, and hidden them, as if they were their own."

Jericho! That's why all this has happened. My thoughts were spinning wildly in my head. Someone had kept some of the gold or silver for themselves, instead of putting it in the treasury.

"I have *seen* what they have done!" thundered the voice. "I *know* what they have done, and who they are. That is why your enemies defeated you today. You will be destroyed by your enemies unless you destroy the person who has done this."

I felt numb. I was shocked. God was so angry.

"Tell everyone to get ready for tomorrow. Tomorrow I will act!"

Chapter Fifteen

I didn't sleep. How could I? I just paced up and down. I didn't bother to put on another tunic. My shredded clothing summed up how I felt. We had brought this on ourselves. Our stupidity. Our disobedience. Who was so full of themselves that they thought they could cheat on God? Who in the world thought that they could do something that God would not know about?

I remembered the time long, long ago when Moses had gone to speak to God on Mount Sinai. I remembered how everyone watched and waited as he went up the mountain, wondering with eager anticipation what God was going to say. But then the people had lost patience. They had built a calf, made of gold, and while Moses was at the top of the mountain talking with the Lord God, the people were at the bottom, worshipping the golden statue.

But God had seen everything. He knew exactly what was going on. Nothing escapes him. And he was very, very angry. Just like he was now.

A burst of anger rose within me too! How could it have happened? It made me speechless. Such arrogance! Such pride! It was unbelievable that anyone who had seen all that we had seen in the last few days should even *think* about disobeying God. Did they really think that the Lord God who had stopped the River Jordan flowing downstream and caused the walls of Jericho to crash down all by themselves, would not know when someone had lied or stolen something from him?

I wondered who it was. Who would do such a thing? I didn't suppose I was the only one awake. Or perhaps they thought they would get away with it.

I sighed. I knew better. God had already told me what to do and how it would end. The thief and the cheat would be caught and punished. There was no doubt that God demanded justice. And he would make sure he got it. It was all to do with his holiness.

Dawn came, but the sky was dark and gloomy. Everyone left their tents and stood with their families, tribe by tribe.

"Tell each tribe to stand before me!" said God.

"Reuben!" I said.

The tribe of Reuben fell to the ground.

Nothing.

"Gad," I said.

The tribe of Gad fell to the ground.

Nothing.

"Judah," I said.

"Judah's the tribe!" said God.

The tribe of Judah stayed on the ground. The other tribes let out a sigh of relief, but nobody felt like talking. We had a long way to go yet.

I called out the names of each family group. As I said each name nothing happened.

"The Zerahites," I said, as I reached the end.

As soon as I had said it, I knew this was the family. I felt myself tremble, moved by the power of God, prompting me.

The Zerahites clung to the ground.

Everyone else moved away.

"Stand before God, family by family!" I ordered.

Zimri's family stood up.

Again, I felt a surge of power and I knew God was telling me that one of Zimri's family was the culprit. Zimri stood before God. Next to him stood his son Carmi, and his grandson Achan.

As soon as I looked at Achan I knew he was the man. "Achan," I whispered. Achan fell to his knees. I walked towards him. Fool though I thought him to be, I couldn't help but feel sorry for him. God knew. God knew everything.

"Tell God what you have done," I said to him gently. "It's pointless to do otherwise. Tell me what happened."

I surprised myself with the way I spoke to Achan. All night I had been thinking of all the things I would say to the person who had done this to us all. Now that I saw who it was, now that I could see his fear, now that I could see how stupid he had been I knew that it wasn't my job to rant and rave. Only God had the right to be angry. Not me. In some ways we were all a bit like Achan. Thought we could get away with things. But we can't, and Achan was just about to find out the hard way.

"Tell me what happened," I repeated.

"All right!" said Achan at last. "I did it! It's true! I have sinned! I have done all the things that God said. I have stolen and I have lied."

You could have heard a pin drop. Nobody moved.

"It was at Jericho," continued Achan.

I knew it! And I had thought everything had gone so well!

"I went into the city with everyone else, and I brought out some treasure, just like you'd told us to do."

Achan paused. He swallowed hard. "It was when I saw some of the treasure, it happened," he said. "I just couldn't help myself. You see there was this beautiful robe. It must have come from Babylonia, or somewhere like that. It was so fine and such a beautiful colour. I had never seen anything like it. The moment I saw it I knew that I just had to have it. I don't think I have ever wanted anything so much. And when I touched it..."

His voice trailed away for a moment. "It was so light. All those years of wandering round in the desert. All those years of nothing much to eat. All those years of such... such..." he struggled to find the word, "... greyness. And suddenly there I was standing amongst such beauty. I put it round my shoulders. There was no one else with me. I thought to myself, what will God want with a robe like this? He'll never miss it. And anyway, I deserve a treat, something special, after all I've been through. We all do. And it was then that I saw the gold and the silver, and I thought that if I was going to take the robe, I might as well take the gold and the silver as well. So, I took them. It was very easy really. Nobody noticed. I took them to my tent, dug a hole and put them inside. And nobody knew..."

"Except... except..." I prompted him.

"Except God," he muttered, and he lowered his eyes.

"Go and find what Achan took," I said to some of the men from the tribe of Judah. I didn't know which was Achan's tent . There were so many of them, after all. But I knew that they would know. They were part of the same tribe.

The men rushed off, dodging between the tents. I knew they wouldn't take long. And I knew they would find the things Achan had taken. I could tell when a man had confessed. Even though he knew he was in trouble, he looked relieved somehow. Relieved that the truth was out.

They brought the stuff to me and put it before me.

"It's not mine," I said. "It belongs to God. Spread it out in front of him."

They did so, laying the beautiful robe over the ground, along with the gold and the silver. There were hundreds of shekels worth of it. Even in the dullness of the daylight they looked magnificent.

"But not worth the trouble it has caused," I said to myself. "Not worth losing your life for."

"You have brought trouble on us," I said turning to Achan.

I could tell from his face he knew what

"Because of what you have done you have brought trouble on yourself. Take him away."

The men took him. And they took the things he had stolen.

Achan was killed. In the end he was buried with the things he had taken.

Chapter Sixteen

The camp was very quiet that night. It was very, very still. Achan's punishment sent a shiver through us all. It was a harsh reminder that we had to take God seriously.

How quickly things had changed since the thrill of the Jericho victory! I couldn't begin to think what would happen next.

The breeze was so gentle I almost ignored it. It was soft and warm, a stark contrast to the icy wind of yesterday.

"Joshua!" said the voice. I recognised it at once. It was the voice of God. It was the voice of God I knew and loved, gentle and loving. And the moment I heard his voice, I knew that it was over. God was no longer angry with us. The price had been paid. God was with us again.

"Don't be afraid!"

I sighed. It was quite hard not to be afraid when you had seen God in action. But I knew what he meant. We didn't have any need to be afraid any more. We'd been punished and forgiven.

"Don't be put off!" said the voice. "You will conquer Ai. I have already made it happen! You will have the same success as you had at Jericho only..."

Only what? I wondered. I really couldn't bear any more uncertainty.

"Only this time take the whole army with you. And..." God paused a moment. I almost felt he was enjoying making me wait. "*This time* you *may* plunder the city and keep what you want. It's yours! But first, you must all set an ambush..."

God knows what he's doing. He has some amazing plans.

We set out at night and camped in the valley. The stars twinkled high in the sky over the huge city of Ai. We watched the clouds. The moment they covered the moon we were ready to go.

I gave the signal to the ambush force, making sure that I followed God's instructions to the letter. I wasn't going to argue with him. Nobody was. Not after what had happened to Achan.

I watched as the men crept off into the darkness across the valley, keeping west of the city until they got into their positions behind it. I lost sight of them as they melted into the darkness, but I knew they would obey my instructions. Once round the other side they were to lie in wait, ready to attack. They knew the signal for the attack. It would come the moment they saw us retreat!

I made camp with the rest of my army and waited in the darkness. We would give the others the night to lay the ambush, and as soon as it was light we would march on the city.

As soon as the golden sun glinted over the horizon we were on our feet.

"Ready?" I nodded to my officers.

They nodded in reply.

"Let's go then! Attack Ai!"

"Quick march!" Left, right, left, right...

We marched on, in a straight line, towards the city gates. We hadn't gone far before I could see faces poking over the top of the walls. They had seen us coming. So far, so good. We just kept going forward. Left, right, left, right...

We hadn't gone far when I saw the city gates open.

"Get ready!" I said to my men over my shoulder.

I heard them pass the message through the ranks.

Suddenly the gates opened wide and out thundered the king of Ai, his troops behind him. They galloped out of Ai, whooping and shouting.

"We're coming to get you!"

Some people never learn!

I let them come towards us.

It was working. God's plan was definitely working.

"Go!" I screamed to my troops as the King of Ai rushed down towards us.

As soon as I had given the order we all turned round as fast as we could, running away from the city.

"Run to the desert!" I shouted. "Keep going! Don't let them catch us!"

"You cowards!" shouted the king. "Didn't you learn your lesson the last time?

Or do we have to give you another roasting?"

I didn't have time to reply. I was facing the wrong way. I was too busy fleeing in the opposite direction.

"Haven't you learnt *your* lesson?" I wanted to say. "We have the Living God on our side.

I pounded forwards, overtaking my troops, feeling the wind flow through my hair, my arms and legs going faster and faster.

As soon as I had gained enough distance between myself and the enemy, I stopped and looked behind me. Hundreds and thousands of men were running after us, their backs to the city.

"I don't suppose there is anyone left to defend the city," I said to God quietly.

"I don't suppose there is," I thought I heard him say. "Now you know what you have to do."

"I do," I said, and faced Ai. I took hold of my javelin and held it high in the air. Slowly I lowered it until it pointed to Ai.

Suddenly I felt a curious sensation running

through me. A shiver ran down my spine, up my shoulder and along my arm like a flash of lightning running through the sky, right to the heart of Ai.

And then, even though I was a long way off, I knew exactly what was happening. My troops would leave their hiding place and conquer the city. It was completely undefended.

"Go on! Go on!" I willed them. There was no time to lose. The king of Ai had almost caught up with us.

Within moments a tell-tale burst of smoke gushed from the city across the sky.

I watched as the enemy stopped in their tracks. They had been tricked. They knew they were beaten. Their city was in ruins. They had nowhere to go. There was no escape.

It didn't take long for us to polish them off. They had lost before they had even drawn their swords.

We took what we needed from the city and then we left.

At last! God had given us the victory!

Chapter Seventeen

I knew exactly what I had to do next. The memories of all that had happened after Jericho were still far too clear in my mind. Just to think about it made me shake. I moved my hand across my cheek and remembered the way I had flung myself to the ground, in front of the Ark of the Covenant, God's presence with us.

This time it would be different.

This time I would do what another leader had done. Moses.

I thought back to the wise old man I had known and loved so well, and I smiled. How pleased he would have been to hear of our triumphs. How sad he would have been when we got things wrong. "He'd have understood," I said to myself. "He'd have known all about it. The same sort of things happened when he was leader. Now that I am leader I must do something Moses would have done."

I left the camp and made my way towards Mount Ebal. There I saw what I was looking for. Scattered at the foot of the mountain were some large stones. These were what I needed.

I carefully selected my stones, dragging some and carrying others until I had put them, one on top of the other, to make an altar. It took some time. Some stones that had at first looked ideal proved to be the wrong shape. Ordinarily I might have hammered away at them, chipping at them until they became the shape and size I needed. But I knew I couldn't do that. Moses had told us so, and I remembered, that the stones had to be uncut. They could not be shaped by a person using a tool, but had to be as God had made them. I shook my head at the thought. I knew the reason why. God knew that we would end up by praising the stonemason rather than him! How well God knew us!

I worked away until the altar was finished. Then I summoned the people together. Everyone had to be there. The priests and the elders of each of the twelve tribes of Israel, every man, woman and child. The young and the old. Even those strangers who lived with us, as one of us, like Rahab and her family. And of course, the Ark of the Covenant was there. There would be little point in doing any of this, if God was not with us.

I took the flaming torch and lit the wood which surrounded the sacrifice. The whole thing burst into flames, and as it did so the people fell to their knees. "Praise God!" they said, as they watched the smoke rise up into the heights of the sky. "Praise God who keeps his promises for ever."

Then, as the people watched, I took two large stones, which had already been prepared to make the surface flat and even. Using two iron tools, I chipped away at the stones, writing the laws that God had given Moses. Writing God's laws that were hidden deep in the middle of the Ark of the Covenant, God's laws which were to be at the heart of God's people, at the core of our new life in the Promised Land of Canaan.

"Listen to God's law," I said in a loud voice, for everyone to hear. "Listen to what God says."

The people stood and listened.

"Love the Lord your God! Do not have any gods other than me!"

"Amen!" shouted the people in return. "Let it be so!"

"Do not make any idols. Do not bow down and worship them!"

"Amen!" shouted the people again. "Let it be so!"

"Amen!" they responded to each of the laws, as I read them from the stone tablets.

Each time I spoke, it was as if the Ark of the Covenant flickered and gleamed in a boost of new light. Even though I was the one who was speaking, I could see that the people were not looking at me. They were looking at the Ark. They were looking towards God. Just as it should be.

When I had finished I turned towards the Ark of the Covenant. "Remember. Everyone remember what God has said. Remember that if we fully obey and follow God's laws, which I have read today, he will bless us and give us every good thing. But if we fail to obey him and follow him, disaster will follow us."

"Amen!" shouted the people and they fell to their knees again. "May God bless us and keep us."

"Yes," I said to the Lord God. "Bless us and keep us, just as you have always done. Help me to be a good leader and to remember all the things you have told us to do."

I stood and faced the people. God's people. My people. We are God's people and he is our God, I thought. I looked again, my eyes darting across the faces of thousands of people, young and old, and I smiled. "God's people and my people," I muttered to myself. "They are my people and I am their leader."

Their leader! The words hit me. Their

leader! And I thought back over all that had happened since Moses had died and I had looked across the Jordan into the Promised Land of Canaan, uncertain and unsure what to do next. So much had happened. So much had changed.

I felt that strange feeling again, of shivers running up and down my back, and I remembered the time Moses had put his frail old hands on my head and named me as his successor.

A gentle breeze flowed round us. Nobody wanted to move. Nobody wanted to break the magic of this special moment as we stood together as a nation, as one family, basking in the feeling of being in God's presence, enjoying being at peace with him.

Looks can be misleading, all right. But as I looked, I could see that for the moment anyway, looks weren't deceptive at all. We were standing together as God's people. For the moment I was their leader. God had given me the strength I needed. He had helped and guided me and I knew that, as long as we kept standing together with God, absolutely everything was going to be all right.

If you've enjoyed this book, why not look out for...

'I didn't feel nervous because I knew that I was doing what the Lord God wanted and he was the one who was really in control. "This is it!" I shouted. My voice boomed across the mountain. "People of Israel, from today you will have to decide who you are going to worship – God or Baal. We'll ask both of them to send down fire from heaven and the true God is the one who sends down fire!"

Elijah tells us what it was like to be one of God's prophets when Queen Jezebel was determined to kill him. At times he was running for his life. But whenever Elijah felt very alone, God had already got a plan in place.

ISBN 1 85999 452 0

Available from your local Christian bookshop

Suddenly the boat lurched sideways and the ropes of the nets creaked and groaned. 'Fish!' yelled Andrew, trying to tug the nets in. 'Help me, Peter!' I grabbed the net and heaved as hard as I could. I felt the boat drop in the

water. We slowly made our way to the shore and the waiting figure of Jesus. He looked so ordinary, just like one of us. And yet I knew he wasn't ordinary at all.

Peter tells us what it was like to leave fishing and follow Jesus as one of his disciples. There were good times and bad times – like the time he let Jesus down. But even after that, Jesus still had a job for Peter to do.

ISBN 1 85999 453 9

Available from your local Christian bookshop

'I can't stand my brother! Do you know what I mean?

It's a shame really, because we're twins. But we're not identical. No way! I haven't got anything much in common with him. He's big and hairy. And I'm, well, smaller – just about right. Yuk! Esau's gross! He's so big and hairy. And he fancies himself.'

Jacob tells us his story. He may have started out as a bit of a wimp but he changed inside with God's help. He even wrestled with God – and lived!

ISBN 1 85999 444 X

Available from your local Christian bookshop